In memory of those who first read to me,
Florence and Jesse Funt
—M.B.

For Teresa
—B.S.

Text copyright © 1994, 2021 by Martha Brenner
Jacket art and interior illustrations copyright © 2021 by Brooke Smart

All rights reserved. Published in the United States by Random House Children's Books,
a division of Penguin Random House LLC, New York. Originally published in significantly different form in the
United States by Random House Children's Books, a division of Penguin Random House LLC, New York, in 1994.

Random House and the colophon are registered trademarks of Penguin Random House LLC.

Visit us on the Web! rhcbooks.com
Educators and librarians, for a variety of teaching tools, visit us at RHTeachersLibrarians.com

Library of Congress Cataloging-in-Publication Data is available upon request.
ISBN 978-0-525-64717-1 (trade) — ISBN 978-0-525-64718-8 (lib. bdg.) — ISBN 978-0-525-64719-5 (ebook)

The text of this book is set in 14-point New Baskerville.
Book design by Sarah Hokanson.

MANUFACTURED IN CHINA
10 9 8 7 6 5 4 3 2 1
2021 Random House Children's Books Edition

ABE
LINCOLN'S
HAT

MARTHA BRENNER · BROOKE SMART

Random House
New York

When Abe Lincoln became a lawyer in 1836, he didn't have much money. He only owned one suit. Yet he wanted to dress like the lawyers he admired. Abe bought a long black coat and a very tall black hat.

Every day, Abe wore his hat to his new job in Springfield, Illinois. People noticed the tall man in the "stovepipe" hat, just as he'd hoped. He was friendly to everyone. When they needed a lawyer, they remembered him. Springfield became the state capital. The highest state court met there. Abe's career grew.

Abe's state was changing. Once, only Native Americans had lived in its woods and on its prairies. Then white pioneers came—with different ideas about land rights. Slowly, through broken treaties, attacks, and harsh laws, the United States forced Native Americans west.

By 1818, when Illinois became a state, more settlers streamed in to build houses and farms and new towns. Sometimes they didn't get along. The settlers argued over land and animals and money. Lawyers like Abe could help them work out their troubles or get a fair trial in court.

Abe Lincoln was a smart lawyer. People came to him with all kinds of legal problems. He helped them all—small farmer or big company.

But he had one problem—he was not a neat paper-keeper.

He was so busy advising people that he didn't update his account books. A good lawyer cannot keep poor records. He was so busy in court that he didn't have time to search his notes. A good lawyer cannot be slow.

He didn't remember to answer letters and he forgot where he put important papers. A good lawyer cannot forget. What could he do?

Abe had an idea. His tall hat! He could push letters deep inside it. He could stuff notes into the leather band. When he took off his hat, the papers would remind him what he had to do or say.

The idea worked, most of the time.

One day, some boys played a trick on Abe. They tied a string across the street. They strung it way up high. Everyone in town could walk under it . . .

. . . everyone except Abe! His hat made him almost seven feet tall! Off it fell! Papers flew everywhere! The boys ran out of hiding. They jumped all over Abe. He was not mad at them. He remembered how little time he'd had to play when he was young, working hard on his father's farm. He enjoyed a good joke.

ALincoln

The boys' trick certainly
did not stop Abe from
carrying papers in his hat!

One time, a lawyer sent Abe a letter, and—as usual—he stuck it in his hat. The next day, Abe bought a new hat. He put away his old one. He always kept a few tall hats—some of smooth beaver fur, others of dressy silk—and a wide casual hat, too.

Weeks later, the lawyer wrote again, asking, "Why didn't you answer my letter?" Then Abe remembered. The letter was still in his old tall hat!

Many towns in Illinois had no lawyers or judges. But each county had one town with a courthouse. So every spring and fall, a judge and some lawyers—including Abe—traveled to these towns to handle cases. Abe always took a tall hat packed with papers. His travel bag held one clean shirt, a few law books, and little else for his long trip.

Until trains linked the towns, the lawyers and the judge had to travel dirt roads and paths on horseback or in horse-drawn buggies. Abe's horse was skinny and slow. Together, they traveled lonely country roads in all kinds of weather.

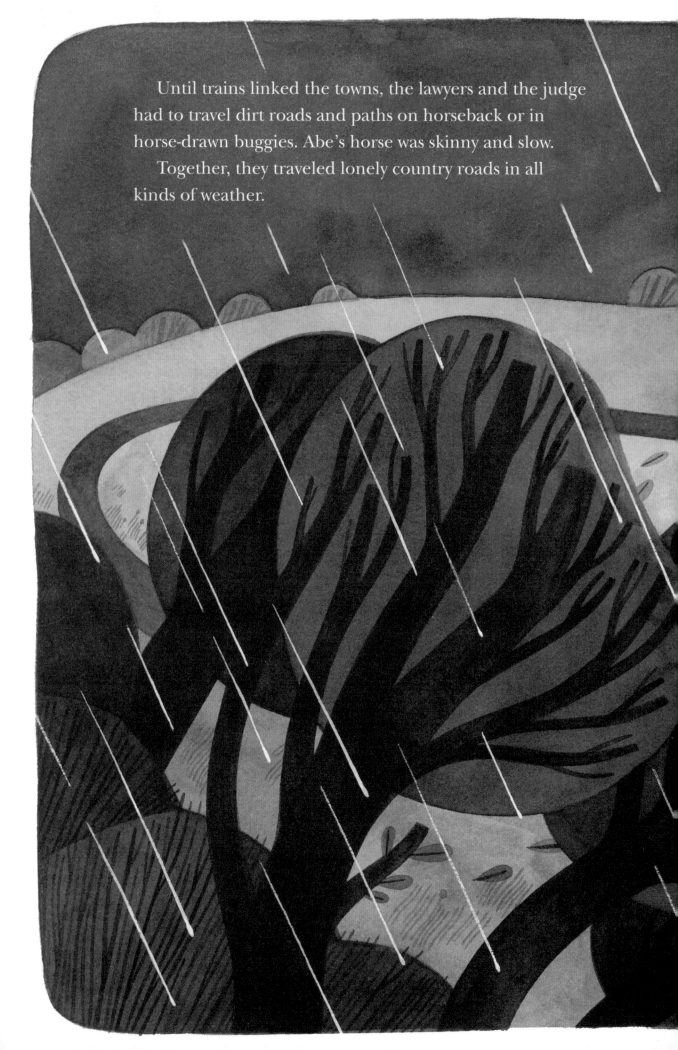

Traveling made Abe weary. He dreamed of a soft bed and a good meal. Instead, the lawyers and the judge often had to stay at poor country inns. The food was bad. The rooms were cold. The beds were crawling with bugs. The lawyers even had to share beds. But the judge, David Davis, got a bed all to himself!

Abe never complained. At the courthouses, he met people
who hired him for new cases. Evenings were spent around inn
fireplaces where he told jokes, talked about law and politics, and
made friends who, years later, would help him become president.

Early in the morning, the courthouse bell would ring. Abe, the judge, and the other lawyers hurried to court. In one small town, pigs lived under the courthouse! Abe had to talk loudly over the grunts and squeals.

People came from near and far to hear Abe. Lawyers admired the way he summed up a case. He made any trial easy to understand. People said he could make a hog laugh with his funny stories and jokes.

If Judge Davis was going to step out, he chose Abe to be his substitute on the bench. The two men thought alike about the law. Also, other lawyers highly respected Abe. "Judge" Lincoln decided over three hundred cases.

In court, Abe used everything he knew, not only law.

From years of farmwork, he learned how to handle horses better than most lawyers. So he knew what to do when two men each claimed to own a young horse.

Abe led everyone out of the courthouse. Each man had brought a mare he said was the colt's mother. Abe put the mares on one side of the lawn, and he held the colt on the other side. Then he set the colt free. It headed straight for its mother, proving who the owner was, once and for all!

From piloting flatboats down the Mississippi River as a young man, Abe learned to steer through dangerous river currents. He used that knowledge when he argued a famous case between a boat owner and a railroad company.

ROCK ISLAND REPUBLICAN

RAILROAD WINS!

HURD V. ROCK ISLAND RAILROAD CO.

A new steamboat, the *Effie Afton*, had crashed into a pillar of the first train bridge across the Mississippi. The boat had sunk in flames. Luckily, no one was killed.

In court, Abe showed how the boat pilot's mistakes led to the crash, and the railroad did not have to pay for the boat. Abe's case won support for railroads to expand west.

Even after Abe became famous, he never forgot old friends. Late in his career, Hannah Armstrong wrote him for help. Abe had lived with her family when he was a young man looking for work. Now Hannah's son Duff was in jail—accused of murder!

Abe did not stick the letter in his hat. He wrote back right away, "Of course I'll help you."

One night, Duff and some other men had been in a fight in the woods. The trees cast dark shadows. But a witness claimed he saw Duff hit a man hard in the head. The injured man managed to ride away, falling off his horse a few times, and soon died.

Duff said he was innocent, and Abe believed him. How could Abe prove that the witness was wrong—or lying? Abe began to study every fact of the case.

"How could you see what happened in the dark?" Abe asked the witness.

"The moon was overhead," he said. "Full and bright."

"Are you sure?" Abe asked again and again.

"Yes," the man insisted.

Then Abe asked for an almanac, a book of facts about the sky and weather. He had cleverly given it to a court officer before the trial. It turned out the moon was low in the sky at the time of the fight! Once the man's lie was revealed, no one believed anything he'd said about Duff. The jury and judge set Duff free.

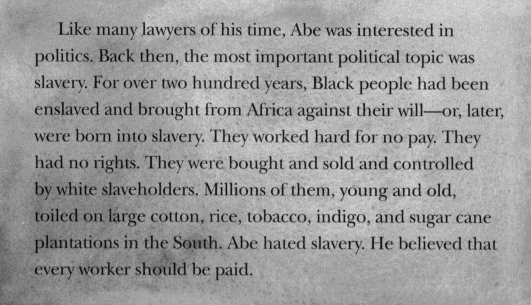

Like many lawyers of his time, Abe was interested in politics. Back then, the most important political topic was slavery. For over two hundred years, Black people had been enslaved and brought from Africa against their will—or, later, were born into slavery. They worked hard for no pay. They had no rights. They were bought and sold and controlled by white slaveholders. Millions of them, young and old, toiled on large cotton, rice, tobacco, indigo, and sugar cane plantations in the South. Abe hated slavery. He believed that every worker should be paid.

PROVISION STORE

Illinois banned slavery but allowed contracts that trapped free Black workers like Nance Legins-Costley into a kind of slavery. Nance's employer, in a hurry to go on a long trip, "sold" her to a storekeeper who agreed to pay $400 for a one-year contract. Her former boss never sent the new contract. He had died while traveling.

When the storekeeper refused to pay the dead man's family, a legal fight began. Nance saw her chance for freedom and bravely quit. She was jailed briefly, but the court case went on for years.

In court, Abe defended Nance's rights. Illinois was a free state, he argued. The sale of free people, whatever their color, was illegal. Nance, without a contract, was free.

The judges agreed. Lawyers used Abe's arguments to free other enslaved Blacks. Illinois soon outlawed all forms of slavery.

Abe had been a young lawyer when he helped Nance. For years after, he took a middle position on slavery. He hoped it could be limited to the South and slowly, peacefully fade away. His ideas about slavery changed over time.

As a congressman, Abe proposed a bill to gradually end slavery in Washington, DC. Few agreed. He voted to prevent slavery from expanding to land won during the Mexican-American War. The plan was defeated.

Abe returned to being a lawyer. Years later, Congress passed a law that allowed slavery in Kansas and Nebraska if settlers voted for it. Abe had feared that slavery would spread.

Then a Supreme Court decision pulled Abe back into politics. The court ruled that an enslaved man, Dred Scott, was *not* free simply because he'd moved to a state and a territory that outlawed slavery. Enslaved people, the justices wrote, were not citizens and had no right to even bring a case to federal court. Abe felt the decision was wrong.

Inspired by past leaders who supported basic rights for *all* men, Abe jotted down thoughts and put them in his hat. Finally, he lashed out in a speech. He called the nation a "house divided." It could not survive "half slave and half free," he warned.

Abe tried to get elected to the Senate. If he won, he would propose laws to stop the spread of slavery. He ran against Stephen Douglas, who argued that each territory should decide whether it wanted slavery. They met for debates all over Illinois.

Thousands of people heard them. Abe lost the election but became well known across America as a gifted speaker and thinker.

In 1860, Abe ran for president. Stephen Douglas ran, too. This time, Abe won!

He headed to Washington with his family and two secretaries, who kept him organized. At every train station, crowds cheered Abe. He had now grown a beard after a girl suggested his thin face would look "a great deal better" with one.

Abe was ready to make his first speech as the new president.
He carried a cane, his speech, and a tall silk hat. He looked for
a place to put his hat. Stephen Douglas stepped up. "If I can't be
president, at least I can hold his hat," he said.

As president, Abe worked hard to unite America again. But his important duties did not stop him from welcoming visitors to the White House or his summer home, often in his favorite slippers!

At the White House, Abe opened his office twice a week to the public. Anyone who wanted to talk to him could get in line. He liked hearing different viewpoints.

Helping someone with a problem made him feel good, too.

Yet even with two secretaries, his desk stayed cluttered. Visitors waited while the president sifted through papers. Usually he found what he needed. If something was *still* missing, his secretaries knew just where to look . . . in his tall hat!

The Lincoln Presidency: An Afterword

By Abraham Lincoln's third month in office, eleven states where slavery was upheld had broken away to form a separate nation in the Deep South—the Confederate States of America. A long civil war began between the Confederates and the Union, with its twenty-five northern, border, and western states. Both sides suffered great losses.

Lincoln's years as a lawyer had taught him to compromise, to accept new ideas when old ideas failed, and to study complex problems. He used these skills to lead the country and manage a war. For the first time, he met famous Black leaders, like the abolitionist Frederick Douglass. They talked as equals. It was time for bold change.

In 1863, to help end the war, Lincoln signed an order called the Emancipation Proclamation, freeing over three million enslaved people in Confederate states. Many of them fought bravely for the Union, alongside free Black men from the North. The next year, Congress approved equal pay for Black soldiers. Lincoln supported an amendment to the Constitution that banned slavery. As Union victories ended the war, Lincoln, now reelected, began to unite the nation. His work was cut short when he was shot on April 14, 1865, and died the next morning. A special funeral train carried him home to Springfield, Illinois. He is remembered as one of America's greatest presidents.

First Lady Mary Todd Lincoln

Judge David Davis

Frederick Douglass

Stephen Douglas

Abe Lincoln's Secretaries

John Hay

John Nicolay

Places to See a Lincoln Hat

A tall hat worn by Abe Lincoln is on display at the Smithsonian National Museum of American History in Washington, DC. Many personal items can be seen at the Abraham Lincoln Presidential Library and Museum in Springfield, Illinois. Visitors can also tour Lincoln's home and office. The piles of papers are long gone, some stored safely in archives.

Sources

Adams, Carl. *Nance: Trials of the First Slave Freed by Abraham Lincoln*. North Pekin, Illinois: CreateSpace Independent Publishing Platform, 2014.

Billings, Roger, and Williams, Frank J., editors. *Abraham Lincoln, Esq.: The Legal Career of America's Greatest President*. Lexington: The University Press of Kentucky, 2010.

Dirck, Brian. *Lincoln the Lawyer*. Urbana and Chicago: University of Illinois Press, 2007.

Duff, John J. *A. Lincoln, Prairie Lawyer*. New York: Rinehart, 1960.

Foner, Eric. *The Fiery Trial: Abraham Lincoln and American Slavery*. New York: W. W. Norton & Company, 2010.

Freedman, Russell. *Lincoln: A Photobiography*. New York: Clarion Books, 1987.

Goodwin, Doris Kearns. *Team of Rivals: The Political Genius of Abraham Lincoln*. New York: Simon & Schuster, 2005.

Photograph Credits